DRY WELLS
OF INDIA

THE
DRY WELLS
OF INDIA

Edited by George Woodcock

AN ANTHOLOGY AGAINST THIRST
Selected Poems Entered in the
Canadian Poetry Contest 1987–88

HARBOUR PUBLISHING

Copyright © 1989 Canada India Village Aid

Harbour Publishing
P.O. Box 219
Madeira Park, BC
V0N 2H0

Cover painting by *Evening Sky, Lake Palace, Udaipur, India* by Toni Onley. Permission kindly donated by the artist.
Cover design by Alex Baggio, Creative Graphics.

Printed & bound in Canada

Canadian Cataloguing in Publication Data

Main entry under title:
The dry wells of India

ISBN 1-55017-001-5
1. Canadian poetry (English)—20th century.*
2. Canadian poetry (English)—Competitions.*
I. Woodcock, George, 1912–
PS8293.D79 1988   C811′.54′08   C88-091646X
PR9195.7.D79 1988

Contents

Introduction

Margaret Atwood

This is not an ordinary anthology of poems. It's a harebrained scheme or a leap of faith, depending on your level of cynicism. It's something that shouldn't have worked, but did. In its modest way, it's the word made flesh.

How can you convert poetry—usually considered one of the most aerial and impractical of human expressions—into a cluster of small irrigation dams in arid parts of India? Dams which will create many seasonal jobs in one of the most destitute areas of the earth and continue life through the provision of water for thousands of people and their animals: an immeasurable quantity of renewed hope. But this conversion of poetry to irrigation dams is what George and Inge Woodcock set out to do. They ran a poetry contest to help sponsor Canada India Village Aid. Each entrant was charged five dollars. The entries were sifted by preliminary judges—George Bowering, George McWhirter, W.H. New and Inge Woodcock—and a batch of 51 poems selected from an astonishing 3,223 entries was then read by final judges Al Purdy, George Woodcock and myself. We selected six winners and one first place. The winners all read at Toronto's Harbourfront Reading Series to, I'm pleased to say, a packed and enthusiastic house. The entrance fees for the contest, the proceeds from the reading and the royalties from this anthology all go to Canada India Village Aid and will be matched three to one by CIDA, generating a total of about $65,000. The money is enough to build about ten small stone-faced dams using village labour.

This may not seem a whole lot of money, but the Canadian dollar goes far in poverty-stricken regions of India. Even so, it may not seem like much, in view of the overwhelming global problems of poverty, the overpopulation of fragile regions, malnutrition, and overuse and desertification of the land which face us now in the late twentieth century. But although these problems are global, the solutions must begin locally or there will be no solutions.

The philosophy of Canada India Village Aid is not free handouts; instead, through its on-the-ground programmes which combine medical services and agrarian advice with small-scale conservation and construction, it strives to help make a village or local area self-sufficient.

For this book, the poems were selected from those which arrived so generously from all over Canada and the United States. They are of an amazing range and variety and represent no one school, no one movement or approach to language, and no one region. All the poems have in common is quality and the goodwill of their authors. We are often told that words cannot really change the world, and by themselves they cannot. But in partnership with human initiative and inventiveness and will, they stand more than a candle's chance in the harsh winds that are blowing over the earth.

Increasingly, the world *is* a village. If the rainforests go, so will our oxygen, eventually. If weather patterns are changed elsewhere, through human neglect, greed or desperation, they will change for us too. Unless we begin somewhere, we will not begin. Unless we help others we will be unable, finally, to help ourselves.

Thus this book.

Editorial Note

George Woodcock

The Canadian Poetry Contest was launched in the fall of 1987 to provide funds that would be used by Canada India Village Aid in its programme of building dams and digging wells to help counter the serious drought conditions that have arisen in north-western India during recent years. By contest deadline of April 15, 1988, a total of 1,255 poets had entered no less than 3,223 poems. The poems were submitted from all the provinces and both territories. They came from Canadians abroad as far away as Brazil, and from foreign poets who were welcome in view of the international nature of the appeal. They came from known and unknown, from younger and elder poets. The present anthology was compiled when we realized that there were many good poems other than those of the six prize winners—John Pass (first prize), J. Delayne Barber, Ron Charach, Jan Conn, Kerry Johanssen and Dale Zieroth—whose work appears at the beginning of this volume.

Margaret Atwood has so admirably sketched in the background of the Canadian Poetry Contest in her introduction and it remains for me to thank all those who have devoted so much time and energy to making the Contest successful: to the judges Margaret Atwood has already named, to Doris Cowan for first printing the winning poems in *Books in Canada* (October 1988), to Howard White for agreeing to publish the present anthology, and to all the poets who so kindly submitted their work and contributed to the bringing of water to parched fields or to thirsty human beings and animals. I would especially like to thank those who allowed their work to appear in the anthology without payment so that the proceeds can go towards relief work.

First Prize Poem

_____

John Pass

_____

Actaeon

A man who surprises the goddess bathing, naked
in full blush, head and shoulders haughty above
her scurrying handmaidens, who stumbles

upon her by accident, in an idle moment
as you or I upon the full, clear moon
over the mountain's white shoulder
driving, some January afternoon
the mundane highway. Such a man

in shift
from man of action to man the actor
in her drama, in transition, on the cusp
unaccountable, inarticulate, awkward
within strident grace

dies at the hands of his companions

dies in the teeth of his training, his prized hounds, dies
her death as image of his desire—wild, elusive
specimen, silhouette
                              on a high ridge, leapt

out of range, out of bounds
                                  except to accident, the tricks
of idleness, subtle art
of intention at rest, of the huntress. He dies

in the noise of his name, his friends shouting
"Actaeon, Actaeon . . .," wondering
at his absence, missing
the thrill of the kill.
And "Actaeon," in tone

innocent, excited
echoes today in its exile (unchosen, undeserved
and not bad luck exactly) echoes

because he cannot answer, strains to
through his muzzle, soft lips, thick tongue
of the herbivore, makes sounds

not animal, not human
and cannot and dies

in a body made exquisitely
for life, a trophy, a transport

for his name, lapsed quickly

on the lips of his companions (never
comprehending) on my lips now

ironic, uncertain, changed as he

who saw her
saw through the guise of modesty and boyish
enthusiasm, her bright body, wet
as any mortal's, saw

through no effort nor virtue nor fault
of his own, his eyes a deer's eyes

darkening, widening, feminine, startled
who otherwise would be unknown to us.

2

Prize Poem

J. Delayne Barber

Narrative Changes

In the old story, she is able. She can move,
inconspicuously in a roomfull of dancers whose steps
are happy. She is everything ordinary and young.

Only the shoes are left, insensible. Visitors arrive
wearing streetclothes, never having spent one day in
distracted isolation. When it all went wrong,

she would remember a day filled with rain, or wind.
Unimportant differences. An afternoon of new distance.
This was not her idea of the scenic route. Ceiling squares,

blood-count. It all adds up to flowered immobility.
A carload of the strictly common, ditched in a country
without maps. After driving to a night of local colour,

nothing strange to tell. Autumn across the hillsides,
pastures of bison, the harvest hayride offer typical
testimony. As a woman of character, she enters each dark

with its morphine sense of motion, plotting
impossibilities. Intensive Care: draw the curtain.
She stages a comeback. Tubes for every orifice,

dripping, draining, maintain the body's balance in its
perimeter of bedside apparatus. The walls blossom
with Get-Well graffiti. Her feet remember their history,

3

thrusting back to the dancehall. The crystal globe
spins its splintered light. Memory lodged in nerve-code
breaks loose like a headless hen. When she wakes

alone, the day is bruised, ice-bound. The floor
does not go unnoticed; poppies fall on it,
and a sleepy silence. Even in good weather this is

dangerous. How much of travel is prior arrangement?
A movement toward beds you will make. Name on the telegram
delivered in the dream you plan to have.

Prize Poem

Ron Charach

Life in the Late Hours

"I fished around inside the bodies
of good dead men, and could find nothing
but my own fear, my own disappointment"

After Midnight in the Gross Anatomy Lab,
cramming

God forbids the middle ear;
you are here to explore only the larger stations,
refusing to see them as they once saw themselves.
Women. Men. In formalin.
On cool metal tables, catch their deaths. . .
Tables so short you might never guess their purpose,
blindfolded. But then, many come from India.
Infant skeletons a major export.
Their organs pulled out for inspection
then put back in their cases. How many
might still play well inside other bodies?
Though, after midnight these dead do get up,
to play tennis,
The Prosects against the Dissects;
at first the Prosects always lose,
—their cut muscles flapping from their bones,
but gradually. . . gradually. . .
the Dissects start losing a muscle here, a nerve there,
pectoralis major, then *minor*,
so if you catch the game late enough in the term

it's a toss-up
who wins.

Scratching with his scissors for fallopian tubes

Searching for life in the late hours,
the rest of the class gone home for the good sleep,
leaving behind their pure white suits
in a pile.
On the particular day they did *the face*
he came down with something,
and had to miss the lesson.
Something in his own body knew that the lipless grins
would forever make watering the specimens
more difficult. Like a game of mime,
warm water trickling through a punched-out spout;
—pretends he's watering plants; his mind
dousing their heads with humour. Vegetables.

Each of Twelve remember

throbbing in the now empty
thoracic cage. And if a cage,
for what variety of bird
that must sing sweetly in love
yet eat its way through meat
for the final escape.
And what degree of animal
must the skull contain.
Twelve well-preserved women and men going bad
their thin beams up in stirrups
a unisex clinic, full of tampon-remover jokes,
whores in the wrong hands. . . .

6

By morning the skylight buys back the room

for the living.
I return to my favourite body, his face
behind the flat green drape.
While his mask was still attached
he wore a long thin reed of a moustache
waxed up at the ends
and was nicknamed The Colonel.
With not one extra ounce of fat,
—must have had cancer.
Yet he is the colonel still, *my* colonel
and acquiescing cadaver;
And when he willed his husk
to teach me, he too
had wanted to rise and meet
the basic science.
Through the silent shroud:
A tear for what we are, and must be,
might still be squeezing through
these tiny twisted canals
even as the two of us
explore—

Prize Poem

Jan Conn

A Tapestry

Backs to the miniature pear-trees
in the medieval herbal garden,
my sister and I goof around,
teen-aged. The pears muscular
as green uteri, unpicked,
untasted.

The leaves are locked in resin
as though in a museum for extinct trees.
Above them our mother sits, cross-legged
on a satin cloud, surrounded
by a crowd of women. She's talking
to us through a loud-speaker,
she's saying, have you killed her yet,
the impostor, the new wife? Have you learned
how to torture your father?

Fighting the drone of a plane
that writes a message in the sticky
blue-seamed sky over the Hudson,
mother talks louder,
her dead mother joins her and then
her only son, alone
among all those women.

It's for him I let go
of my sister's hand, climbing up
on the stone wall

warmed by September,
past the comfrey and gold of pleasure,
St. John's wort and fennel seed,
and the nuns building gigantic nests,
like storks,
beside the tombs of the crusaders.

Prize Poem

Kerry Johanssen

The Listening Perch

I

At the edge of a pine clearcut, a horned owl shifts his weight
from claw to claw on a snag birch

He hears the shrew creep under the earth, hears the vole
steal up toward moonlight

When the vole rubs topsoil, the owl stiffens his spine, wings flex,
tail feathers flip

The owl sweeps toward the pulse, his clawed leg jams the
        tunnel,
flinches once

Wings beating a tense hover, he draws the small life to his beak,
clips the nerve from the skull

II

My father is a child blowing a duck call through the night

Squawks, chortles sprawl in wind behind the muffler
His father's Stetson brushes the roof of the Ford

The back seat has melons, strawberries, crates of peaches
The trunk reeks of salted pelts, white mink, raccoon

An owl shatters the windshield, hits the boy in the chest,
a vole flops into his father's lap

Dawn at Lake Saline, they cut the bird for catfish bait
A black lab swims after the boat, down clings to his muzzle

III

Smell of formaldehyde
I stand on a chair, peer down into a woman's belly

My father jokes with his German nurse Helga, I keep hearing
        Bach
stream from his hands, a fugue I play

In the dark, feeling for sounds
I don't understand the jokes or the ovaries but I laugh

The knife clips them out
He tells the story of hunting teal off the coast of Cameron

The woman looks dead but her breasts heave

Mudboat stuck on a sandbar, tornado snaking over the Gulf,
pluming the marsh up and down in a waterspout

He prayed under a shrimp barrel when the eye sucked his
        breath
Hours practicing knots, not touching

When bodies lie still and won't get up, it's hard to believe

Helga nods *Ya bitte* with every joke and I keep tapping
Bach on my fingertips

IV

This moon brings a scent of orange rind
It hovers, this groan of a trunk dried by lightning

My lover reads a history of cure rates in Bedlam
I hammer chords, keep my heart alive

He sneaks up behind me, his hands flinch
My lover, a sweet lie on the tongue

Orange rinds float on the pond and there is no metaphor

Crack of tree rings, hushed impact on ground cover

———————

Dale Zieroth

———————

The Death of the Violin

. . . in our house came after four years.
She had practised—and not practised—
long enough to (finally) make music.
She had entertained my father and mother,
and I had been proud of the songs
she had coaxed from those harsh strings.
She was, however, not staying with it.
We could no longer continue with
reminders, because reminders would be
nagging, and we wanted discipline
on her part: we wanted her to bring her will
into play.

November is a hard month to give up anything,
especially if you have held it
four years, watched it grow in your arms,
until you knew just how
to make the music leap.
My own father's violin hangs on the wall
and I remember when he played,
touching the strings, jabbing
at the notes until the instrument
became a fiddle, and around him
guitars and accordians
filled up the family with their talk.

Once, when she played,
his violin played back,

reverberating on the wall: just once
there was that calling note. Then silence.
Filled up now with rain,
with arguments about who's supporting whom
through this decision—they last their time
and fade, but stay, fill the air
and are cast back slowly into the pit
of all old family fights,
where the world gets drained off to
when it lurches and
can't move gently into change
and someone's disclaiming all reason
and another's volume rises to the shriek.

Rod Anderson

The No-Sayer

upstairs our neighbour has a new dog
no   he says to her all day long   no
sometimes rising in warning   nooooooooo...
other times the descent of surprised pain   noooh!
an appeal to gentle reason   nnnno   and when that fails
staccato commands for discipline
no! no! no! no! no!
riddling our ceiling   ratatatat
the pup herself we never hear
just now the faint squeak of a chair   garbled

    amazing be the ways of a talldog
    (I do mention this for dogs who like research)
    his motions be random and unpredictable
    calling ever for foot-dodge worry-eye
    yet at heart I do believe an honest fellow
    neither skimping on pats nor meat-nibbles

    only it be his language falls strange upon the ear
    all of one syllable seeming
    lacking the simplest alteration of bow to huff to yap
    (take all my crunchbones if this be not true)
    for always from his mouth this one repeated sound

    after much study I have divined its meaning
    which be simply: he is still and I moving
    for whenever these two conditions be met
    no's issue from talldog's mouth like magic

(scarce weaned I am   untutored
yet have I not grasped the knuckle of it?)

this be a good game I think
and now be his turn   his turn
no for thee!   I stand still and wait
no   I try to say   for him to get the idea
but he sits there ignorant
no thyself!   I try

but cannot get the tongue around it

Karen Bodlak

Snow in Six Parts

The memory-bank has melted.
Flakes return,
startling inventive
season and
eureka! we discover
it's redesigned
the earth.

Two at a bus stop
trace out
territory
with boot heels;
like dogs they scar
the raw white fabric.

Bamboo leans
with icy
gravity; the world
weighs more.

Night sinks between the flakes.
We sleep—bees
in the crevice of a white
magnolia flower: ephemeral
hibernation, while drifts
fold in and in and in
upon the house.

Voices
lift like snow-birds
through the heaviness
and settle.
Along the walk our bodies
wade and flounder—we
the elegant
species.

It begins again—slow
and gracious burial; inverse death.
Snow enshrined before
passing,
epitaph pared from
sweet water and sky.

Mick Burrs

Variation on a Poem by Kabir

Although I know God is within me
why am I still
a puffed-up piece of rice?

One day I will throw my cleverness
into the nearest garbage can.
Words brilliantly knotted
cannot tie me to God.

I will not be taken in
by scriptural tyrants and slaves
though they pound on the doors of my ears
and break open the sashes of my eyes.
The truth cannot be grasped
simply by turning pages.

It is the castle of love I seek.
Only my heart's inner river
will guide me there.

> O man, if thou dost not know thine own Lord,
>   whereof art thou so proud?
> Put thy cleverness away: mere words shall
>   never unite thee to Him.
> Do not deceive thyself with the witness of
>   the Scriptures:
> Love is something other than this, and he
>   who has sought it truly has found it.

> Poem I.52 as translated by
> Rabindranath Tagore in
> *Poems of Kabir*, 1915,
> Macmillan of India

Mary E. Chaif

Sound Track

Somebody loves the mud

I saw his size-ten track
in the flower bed

under the leafless
rain-soaked tree
by the flooded path.

No need no need and yet
he did step in
for the sudden lurch

the downward squish
the upward suck of mud!

I saw him pause to see
indentations filling up
before he moved away

his shoulders sodden
light

I wish him well—
I share his swift delight
in simple things.

Dorothy Farmiloe

Five Ways to Outclass Younger Skiers

Together we strap on our skis,
ours familiar and tough as the season itself,
and start down the trail. Behind us
the voices of the younger skiers clutter
the air. We sing at the top of our lungs
to drown out their quarrelling.

If they'd listen to us, if they'd
give us some credit for distances logged—
our skis after all have seen more tours
than they have years—
but no, they ski right through us
as if we don't exist.

If they think of us at all
it is with amusement that we still
maintain an interest in the game.

What do they think we do with our time—
sit in separate rocking chairs? We split
that misconception into kindling years ago
and built a roaring fire with the pieces.

We eat granola with our toast.
We spike our tea with rum.

We dazzle the winter sun
by stripping and making love on each hill
up ahead. We cry *Look, Look*. They still

don't see. But one day they will remember
we were here.

Joan Finnigan

This Is the Lair of a Primitive Man

This is the lair of a primitive man

he is
a loud voice
holding court in the kitchen
of the universe

he hullabaloos daily happiness
sometimes heard at the foot of the mountains
even in fox dens and in bear caves where beasts
still hide from the wild men
of Quebec

he stays,
he stays on his land for generations
and he is everywhere;
in tall men's tales told in kaleidoscopic bars,
in the knots of traps forgotten in the thinning woods;
genie-like he leaps in the memories of starving widows
looking out windows at overgrown pastures

a love-child
conceived in the hayfields of philosophy
he did not need to attend a school
for he was born telling stories,
speaking poetry;
from his fathers he knows the names of all
the trees, and how well they fire;

he has never longed to leave the world

his jaw is set on tribal unforgiveness,
he has explored miracles and step-danced on dreams,
he closes every day with the same heathen prayer,
he has seen the sun set in the east

even now, mending himself by tricks of will
learned from the Walker in the Snow,
he lolls in the shadow of God

and his hands smell of women

Merci Fournier

Dark Holdings

The well, the drop into the
black hole in this girl's
mind. Tall beech trees where
a brother, climbing saw what
must become a miracle, the
small girl clamouring at
the bottom of the well.
These are her feet, her only
mode of transport, they are
caught in the big iron spike
the love hole, this is the small
end of the world which is barely
begun, this bargain basement
could it really have happened?

In the stench of well, dark holdings,
the life ebbed a little, this
time was the end of the first part
of a dance of death, the small girl
reeling as the stopcock leant against
her feet, the two feet dancing round
the iron point, the dark green slime
as her hands massaged the walls, the
round brick facing her at each turn,
the flailing and the hair or was it
weed in her mouth and all the beech
trees above were silent statues in
her burial.

The girl in the depths of the
well spat her water, her own, the
second time, the first time had
been birth when fluid flowed through
her mouth, nostrils, made her body
quiver with excitement. This second
birth, the well, not quite clean enough
to be recognised, the beech trees
standing so aloof one would have
expected this, everybody praises them
but on this occasion, this dreadful
occasion, they were there with their
smart leaves rustling.

The well, with its dreadful manifestation
sunk in its own holy ground, this is
the spot where second birth portrayed
itself, the marrying of child and
despondency, the dreadful black walls
and the beech trees. Through her teeth
the water, the strong odour of dampness,
the second world.

Mitra Foroutan

Prisoners

I

"Down with the Shah!" he cried
and down he went
into the courtroom
and torture chambers
and jail
and death.
No one uttered a word
when his family disappeared.
There was only
the sound of my grandmother
whispering for us to be silent
and to drink our sweet tea.

II

Silence
was all that was heard
after the thousands like him.
And now she covers herself
but not in shame
as she waits in line
like a soldier
for tea leaves
and for sugar.

Kathy Fretwell

The Beholder

Burning tip of cigarette
transforms slanting sunrays
into teal arabesques.
This interior-decorated air
—dust motes given colour, shape, movement—
matches the weave of my blouse.

Non smokers miss this impromptu
spectacle, gratis of my vice—
as if, aware of elm blight, stagnant ponds,
and wasted blackberries,
nature trusts smokers
—lighting up and resting butts on rock—
to notice on top of creek slime, a sunlit bluebottle.

Susan Glickman

Furniture Polish

Today my hands smell of labour—
garlic oil rubbed into the whorls of the fingertip,
oil of lemon into the grain of the wood.
Odours of mortality, of steady use, the ghostbody of action
like the sweet musk of your skin before your bath
or your faded flannel shirts
into which I press my face when you're away too long, husband.
Strange name I never thought to say in this life,
from the Old Norse by way of Anglo-Saxon, *husbonda*, freeman,
a person owning his own home and therefore in later usage
one who tills and cultivates the soil.
Later still the correlative to wife, sexual partnership almost
an afterthought
or adjunct to the community of house and land.

Similarly with *huswyf*, a woman who manages a household,
especially one who does so thriftily and well—the property
took precedence. Logical if unromantic,
at least to modern lovers holding as they do that love
comes first and conquers all, even garlic
and sweat and unswept floors. The random dazzle
of the idea precedes the particulars
for us; thus the word *husband* became a possibility
on my tongue, and only then could I imagine the stubborn
dailiness of this alliance,
which one bends to eventually and caresses
as one caresses the known grain of an old family chair.
Things made lustrous with use earn this devotion
from us, inspire hope that, with time, we too
may deserve such love.

Martha Gould

Calling the Planet Earth

The sea is the big thing here;
we forget that, calling the planet
Earth. Dolphins from birth
must know this old rotundity as
Water. Nothing flat about it
but the surface on a very calm day,
before the dolphins crease it chasing
squid and sunbeams, leaping
from one ocean's element through
the ring of the other, just
for the hell of it and the air.

They aren't defined by any linear;
are free of the terrible responsibilities
of gravity; have no barns to push
down the road and no road, instead
leading lives of exuberant gaiety.

Desperate only in tuna nets,
or when driven on shore.

Can't count money with a flipper
or a tapered nose; why want to,
anyway?
What's the good of being a man?
they might say, frolicking around
the ferry boats carrying us for a fee
from one little island to the next.

They know nothing of blossoming lilacs
in the interiors of continents,
unless returning birds tell them something
of places where water is constricted
and has no salt in it.

Streamlined for fluidity,
centered in affinity,
acknowledging an ancient
oceanic consanguinity,
an alien though mammalian
enthusiastic equanimity

with a slap-happy flick of
their tails and a grin
on their smooth faces,
with a world of wealth and time
for developing all the true graces:
love and dancing, play and conversation,
and inquiring, just curiously,
into all the wet corners of the creation,
and admiring the moon
as it floats by like a jellyfish
through phosphorescent night

and singing until the sea
resounds with their voices

calling the planet earth

Elizabeth Gourlay

Spectre

Evil has its own Face   a face we know   always have known it

Medes Persians the Hebrews knew it   Hezekiah told it
the Thing terrible   voracious   destructive

there, in the quick silver mirror, the quivering water
goes the hog-snout   small-eyed   long-headed

red mouth dripping   teeth laser sharp   white belly rolling
forever on the move
                    every hour more destroyed bodies
                    every hour more ugly Sharks on the increase
                    ravening. . .

and what of the Other?
Face   wide   gentle   smiling
Fish who exchanged the land for the sea
Dolphins who suffer small children to ride on their backs
remember Opononi
the Gentle who hear sounds high and beautiful
beyond the hearing of humans

down through the ages
these dissimilar faces engraved on
a multitude

Janus two-headed
God with his adversary

we humans are carvers
we choose our reflections

Eldon Grier

The Last Train Stop before Edmonton

spare and blond
fiftyish perhaps
exuberant survivor

Ken my husband in an
Edmonton hospital she says
it seems already minus a leg
he fell and broke its stump
in several places
            nothing I can say

worked still works for the CNR
but here we have our farm we
could never live in town
we've always loved the country
            nothing I can say

lake and vine of smoke
distant concrete to our right
she turns to talk of oil
gas   peat moss   coal
massive shovels (English made)
fishing through the ice
            nothing I can add

workers over there she points
are zipped to job—it seems
against their will—by helicopter

they just don't seem to like it
        nothing I can say

heating here? I've always loved it warm
I like to keep my house at
72 degrees she smiles
        nothing I can say

June Harrison

Faller

I walk along the tree,
remember the top
against the light,
touch the dry branch
that cracked hard, the twin alder
on its way down, and
the Heron leaves,
calls high,
calls high, and I
walk along broken tree.

Connie Hawke

Granny Did It for Posterity

Take archaeologists—
Some guy spends 30 years digging holes in the ground
He sifts, dusts, goes blind
From staring at little pieces of pottery
And fragments of bone under a microscope
Goes mad trying to fit pieces of jigsaw puzzles together
He grows old in a hole in the ground
In some hot desert or cold mountaintop
And for what?
A piece of crockery
Someone used to cook with
A long time ago.

Guess my old granny knew what she was doing
When she lived on the farm, eh?
When a cup or plate or saucer got broken
She'd toss it over the stone fence
At the edge of the bush,
She knew, I tell you—
She was doing it for posterity.

Mapping the Passage

*In 1845 Sir John Franklin with a crew of 129 officers and
men sailed from England to map the Northwest passage
and to collect specimens of arctic wildlife. His ships the*
Erebus *and* Terror *were last seen in July of that year. In
1856 an expedition commissioned by Lady Jane Franklin
found proof of Franklin's death and the loss of his men; an
official diary exhumed from a cairn on King William Island
also described the survivors' plan to walk south to the
mainland. Evidence shows they pulled a life-boat loaded
with food and flammable materials overland for hundreds
of miles before the last men died. . .*

In blade-silver straits between islands even summer
was stillborn, endangered as the adamant songs
of gulls deserting into fogs above the passage

they did not discover. Twin ships lashed by anchor cords
indivisibly to their extinction. Well-crafted hulls
scuttled, crushed by shards of puzzling ice, sharp white as the
    un-

marked fringes of maps, or fine English timbers
bleached and bleaching ivory under the blind-
folded hills. A certain shade of white but not

the white of certainty, that fabric of a virginal century's
premise, torn. White of the whale, winter's bones
scrimshawed with piercing weather. *The Erebus. The Terror,*

the terror. To see that tone stare at the page's edge until snow-
blind as the sailors at their dying, staggering
south into gales, white of blizzard hail cracked shorestones and

this
untouched sheet
of ice, as I fill its pale
                    (white
whalers peering from the foredeck
of search boats into the freezing)
                              surface
with terms of unlikely rescue . . .

                        Sir John Franklin sailed with a

    cargo
                                    of proofs
and charts mapping the misty transition
from history to incoherence;
                        on his maps
a white fiercer than uncomposed parchment
a mutinous pallour, unshrouded cautions
of all colours spread outward like a blot, and hinted

there is no passage here for men
from Devon and Somerset
who have healthy sons and delicate
faithful wives
Whose whole world will become a margin
clenched white around their ships—

                        John Franklin did not discover his aim

but a whiteness in every sound as patient
and impartial as icebergs
awaiting the blind
century sailing onward, credulous, captained by a sane
faith in progress
that read meaning into every passage

because it was sailing ahead too fast, an evolutionary
defect

                                              dust
                grinding the littoral under heads
where gravestones of three men face north like sentries
across a frozen sound
with no one left to inform
of anything

                        a hundred more who scrawled
a linear history
in snow and cairns stuffed with rope and empty tins and polished
bones a cold summer south to Victory
Point

                        then perished
in duned waves
Britannia never ruled, refuted

                                        by blinding storms
the hoar
                face of a spreading earth
hauling behind them a life
                                boat full of England

able in the end
to lift around them with only voices
a fleeting shanty
of song

Alison Hopwood

A mark remains
(Remembering Peggy)

Illness and pain became her portion
her themes   Her need: sympathy
Days weeks and months the same
Sadness settled over her
and then she died
leaving to survivors their regrets
A time to meet is not put off a day or week
looking ahead is past   now is lost in never

> In a crowd of shoppers
> before my eyes   a man falls down
> a burly stranger lies there flat
> gathering on-lookers   Someone kneels
> begins to breathe for him
> Of no use   I turn away
> lose myself in the confusion

Twenty years since we first
said "Come for tea"   exchanged books
took Spring breaks together

We phoned often   shared
confessions and complaints
flew to London once

> Driving along I glance aside and see
> by the road's edge two dogs racing my car
> both at one pace   full stretch

though slower than the car
and going backward in my sight

One evening last August we stood
where the Fraser delta ends
where the river leaves the land for the sea
watched the sun setting
At our feet   the muddy tidal flat
left by the ebb   To the south
the light-ship winked its warning
West and north   horizon to zenith
the sky was red and gold
the dark mountains beyond the city
closing the view

Then I drove her home   Thanks she said
a lovely time   Yes lovely thanks I said
Goodnight   Goodnight
She waved from her door and was gone

October—the cooling days contract
apples fall from the tree
Where each parting took place
a small mark remains

In darkness the year begins
going round again
but not to last August

Charlotte Hussey

If the Self is a House

If the self is a house I have searched for a home.
I have driven country roads past farmed
plots of land shelved against hills,
and mansions silvered with fountains, and shacks
surrounded by garbage and barbed wire.
I have feared for those the wind blows through,
plastic flapping over window holes, as the wind
rushed walls of splintered wood,
buffeted pale siding that clattered and shook
like a sleeping animal disturbed by its dreams.

I have visited flats where the rain leaked in;
I have smelled the moldy signature of the weather,
the slow sadness of things crumbling beyond repair.
I have opened closets whose secrets
were muddy boots and lavender and clothes
stiffened like corpses. I have unlocked armoires
of dirtied costumes, fingered
the polished grains of their blond wood.

From a hallway pierced by the cries of a cat,
I have peered into rooms where men slept
with blue blankets pulled·over their heads like shrouds.
Turning away, I entered the kitchen scattered with bowls,
flour, cabbage, and carrots peeled for soup,
kitchen of stark light that hurt my eyes,
harsh kitchen where no mess was allowed,
that drove me underground
to the dirt floors, rows of paint tins and rusty

tubs, walls of hard sand, of cold stone,
the sudden smells of hemp,

of caulking compound where a small girl sits,
squatting down, holding a fragrant piece
of hairlike rope, sits forever, waiting
for her father to come and repair the shutters,
paint the furniture, fix all that is broken.

Canyon del Diablo

It looked like some kind of hydroponic experiment
a great rolling rich field of green alfalfa
smack in the middle of an arid wasteland

We had a talent for getting lost that day
looking for Canyon del Diablo
trying to find a waterfall
in 100 degree heat and dust
We were told the falls was so high
it hurt your head to stand under it

There was a lot of sand and ocotello
and always the mountains in the distance
but we couldn't find the entrance to the canyon
and now in this Eden of alfalfa
I was going to have someone draw a map

The horses moved away from the van,
looked wild from the corners of wide eyes
The old vaquero spit on the sand,
stood unmoving near the gate
coiling a thin rope

I stepped down and said
Conoce Canyon del Diablo?

He nodded, pointed to the north

Dibuje un mapa, por favor
I held out a paper and pencil
like offering him a coral snake
the way he stepped and turned his head

Que direccion, I said

He looked warily at my outstretched hand
launched a stream of saliva at his feet
then dropped to his haunches,
picked up a gnarled twig

Nosotros estamos aqui, he prodded the dust
then scratched a long line
Rancho Santa Clara, he said
making an X in the sand
Lago arido, and he made a wavy line

As he talked I thought how curious
trusting to dust what he refused
to allow a page and pencil

But he was an old man
and land was all he really knew
He took his food from it
slept on it, danced on it
He made love on it and wept on it
And he embraced it with the countless
furrows of his cracked skin
So it was only natural
when he wanted a thing to be understood
it was the land itself that would tell it
just as it had told everything he now knew

I copied the map onto the paper
It wasn't much different from the one I had
but somehow the ageless device

of carving landmarks into earth
seemed to make the knowledge more graspable

Before we left I mentioned the waterfalls
Hay una cascada alli, I asked him
The old man spit and lifted his shoulders
pretending not to understand

We found the canyon without looking at the map
and after two hours climbing stones and boulders
stood at the trickling source of a seven inch falls

and I marvelled to think the old vaquero
was down there in the valley
somehow knowing where I was,
knowing the need to hurt my head on water

he standing on his map,
on his Canyon del Diablo
just as hot and dry
and sliding off his dusty shoe,
a thin stream of spittle

Norman Liu

pure wisdom: the raincoat

i've no trade to offer you
—but i remember the
glow-nights in my harvest-room,
the light from the white candles
and i was sweet-toothed then,
and i spoke to the gloss in the tablecloths

i've no trade
to give you—
but i remember where
the sun thundered in my ribs,
i could tell you tales of the collarbone days
green-lipped, lean-calved in the slanted
corridors, fleeing-smiled in the velvet hallways
riding home in the mintshadows,
i could see
the emerald dash-board, set in
the diamond city

i have no angled trade—shoe-smelling
and wrapped in green
i have none
i never had one
i could not deny the summers
the mirkwoods and the spiderwebs
—who've no trade either
and the city is a city now. how skillful the growth!

i've no trade
to catch your gaze
but you might be so happy, if only you listened
to my cheekbones
my dark ribs
wet hair
emeralds
you might even cry

Dorothy Livesay

Concerto Heroico: The Quick and the Dead

i

When   after drought
weeks of it
grass brittles
geraniums hang
stiff paper heads
suddenly at dawn a cloud
smudges the sun
rain whispers over shingles
on the roof
crickets needle the air
gulls scream

Then   by noon
all's gone
heat blisters   the brain

It is then   when
blare of trumpets
military missiles
it is then   when
thunder crashes

That solitary sentinel
is ripped in half
at gunpoint
ranks of soldiers
collapse   crumple

in the humped   straw houses
villagers huddle
then flee
dragging their children
by the hair

ii

Who is it
is left stranded
crouched in a hollow?
A woman is there
her breasts pulsing
with unsucked milk
her eyes bulging
from stinging smoke
a wind whines softly
through her tangled hair
How many days
must she stay prone
in a blind stare?
How many days
before a mechanical hand
waves the signal
a whistle pierces
the choked air
dead children curl
petals burning
beneath fire's tongue

How many years
before all is dung
under a huge blue
stone-blind moon?

iii

Lone man

He possessed
a certain power:
legs
that would not break
soles of feet
uncalloused
he walked
    walked
        walked
half way across
the round earth
for peace
and remained
upright

They noosed him though
a tight rope
around his neck
like a colt
he was caught
then strangled
we see his feet
flying on wings
across the desert
sand
a gull's
imprint
forever written
there
The message
clear

Peter Lord

Riding Shotgun in the Twilight Zone

1

Riding shotgun
in the twilight zone,
hugging the cliffs
where the bottom
is forever

2

It's gone electronic
these days, just a
faint hiss of microchip,
whispers of ghosts
chattering through systems
instantly ancient, wisps
disappearing into the disposable

3

Sucker-punching winds
nimble as nitroglycerine,
a sudden shower soaks
ice flakes like hawks
circling down, I check
my powder
and watch the treeline

4

Bad times breed
bad lines; cauled faces
pinched cell-block white
ancient flesh soured and
scattered behind rocks
armed with memories
of somewhere else. This
is dangerous country and
most people pretend
to be leaving;
terrified wagon trains
curled in shadows
praying for a moon
on the outskirts of
the rustle of something
not so nice. Time is
forever too,
after sunset
in this place,
and leisurewear
is frowned on.

5

Caterpillar treads jag
ragged across the
sterile landscape, a skirmish
here, traces of pain
evaporating, a low mewl
under a dead lamppost,
the scrape of vanishing
noise, a return to the redundancy
of horror. Accurate forecasts
are tricky at the moment,

a sudden gesture from a stereotype
could prove fatal.

6

Molasses through clouds:
the caravans move
by instinct, a wrong turn
along a neural path
changes curtains, scenes
shift like zippers
chasing stragglers; a vacuum
is just another place
to visit unnoticed, nothing
to talk about.

7

Rust and explosives, the perils
of the road, like
thirty day notes
in February
they're always there
hanging from the mirror
saying hello. Drops of
indians on the horizon
too far away
to tell
waiting patient, certain
in the dust
in the distance. Metaphors
tend to be western
in this particular
corral.

8

Tendrils of motion
scrape the eyes; like
fingernails on fabric
dancing out of sight
on borrowed time, like
owlhoots in the outfield
stitched with sunlight and
shagging lazy flies, as soft
as spearmint tongues at midnight
the day before
the lynch mob. Acute phobias
lurk behind
more than every bush
on this plateau
of heat-waved cactus.

9

The mirage
like the wart on the
illusion, it drifts
into range, a cemetery
under sail, groping
for a place
in the scheme of things,
a sense of direction
idling in a saddle bag.

10

The clarity
of the edge
of the razor; this vision

strangles through canyons,
desperate yodels clamour
behind a trace of moon, like
children on fire, leaping
over sunken eyes, a gristled sun
burning overhead like
a grinding fever, merciless
and efficient. This trail
has no breaks, not a moment
of memory
to spare, bleak and deadly
a recipe to follow
for travellers riding nightmares.

Anne Marriott

The Lake

My mother went in first
her thin white hair
a mist on the dull water.
My husband floated on his back
as he used to swim
but made no motions.
The water opened for him
like an envelope.
My father dived in boldly
certain there was an outlet.
My dog swam with all his strength
gave out suddenly
a wave filling his blind eyes.
And all the others—my first
music teacher
her stiff black turning sodden—
my uncle
determined to avoid
the queen's telegram of congratulation—
my dear friend
who to the very last
saw *frozen fire* burning where the lakes are ice.

This lake is muddied.
At the shallow end
thick pale weeds
wait to snake out
pull me down with the others.
I keep well back.

(This morning
all around the verge
the water's rising).

Ron Miles

Glenda, Morning

Expecting her father's death
and in forty years her own
she sits in the livingroom still
as though her mind were not
a battlefield. There is no time
for anything, and nothing but time.

Wanting to know we are here
for a reason, and what it is,
she studies the red amaryllis
long past its fullest bloom
shrinks into its core and sacrifices
browning petals, brittle stalk.
All of her talk is gloom.

Even the sky agrees.
Clouds fold in her lap
the air is grey so soon
as her hair, daily
betraying her. Leftover
thunder rumbles behind a ridge
she'll never climb
there is no time

for anything she wants
is out of reach, and nothing
but everything will do. Later
she will rouse and call herself
a fool, but no one will answer—

not father or lover
mother or thunder—
her fears for her children
and our need.

Judy Millar

riding down from budhanilkanth(a*

riding down from budhanilkanth(a
chinese flying pigeon
ordovician bicycle
black joy in metal wrapper
pre-silurian post-cambrian
knees open open to
devonian and
after

green paddy
rice pool brush
thigh
electric kiss by
triassic fish
and back back there
paleozoic post-remembered
like this electric fish
jumps up mesozoic

riding riding down from budhanilkanth(a
lower epoch-bump after
chrome knuckle chrome
tingle up into cretaceous
cretaceous mmmm cretaceous
tongue lover yum
tongue tongue lick
wind

tertiary tertiary
wheels speak laugh flow
tires glow new air
happy for two rupees sly
shy smile
air two rupees mister only two

goodbye goodbye they call
coming and going
paleocene eocene oligocene
miocene pliocene
now now pleistocene
and that means quaternary
goodbye hello it
doesn't much matter
for air two rupees maybe three now
with inflation

budh budhanilkanth(a
sleeping there ago under flowers
dreaming
dead
it doesn't much matter

*Budhanilkantha (sometimes pronounced without the final syllable "a") is a
sacred site on a hill high above the Kathmandu Valley whose focal point is an
enormous stone image of Vishnu (the "sleeping Vishnu") lying prone atop the
snake Ananta. The whole rests in a sacred pond, symbolic of the primordial
waters. Between two world-periods, only Vishnu, the Preserver, exists and he
is asleep. The coming of a new world is signalled when from his navel, a lotus
rises, upon which Brahma, the Creator, appears.

Susan Musgrave

One Evening, the Wind Rising, It Began

raining. I peeked out from behind the blinds
while the lights blinked and my mother went
from room to room in her silence, lighting
the few candles. Flowers on their drunken stems
were opening themselves like brides, and I tried
to explain to my daughter how she couldn't go out
and play any longer in that garden.

Tears fell like spring rain down her face
when I said I thought death might be something
we could return from as another life.
She didn't want to hear this and pushed me
away. She said she wanted to be herself,
always. She wanted me, too, to be who I am.

I have reached an age where even a spring
rain falling on the spring ground can make me
less of what I am. So I told her then what I've tried
to believe in my life, that we don't have to die,
ever. Victorious she turned to me, like the flowers
of this world, the brilliance sliding from her.

A.L.E. Nightingale

Aganetha Against the Wind
(Lines on Paging Through the Family Albums)

    Seemed some wind was always about carrying up
Slip, skirt and apron, big gust catching
At the black flapping of her coat. All that
Sideways tug and drift took her billowing thighs
And midriff almost elsewhere,—everyway
And on any fair and grey day.
    Always the sculpted skull and old features fixed
Fast, tied tight under chin—kerchiefed
Against the click and blast, set
And scowling in black and white for the killing camera.
    And leading in the rather more photogenic
Heavy-horse and plough, humped hoeing a row
Or following the pretty cow out, she was all spit
And stamina. Her bow-legs in those heavy hose
Stood planted firm. (And still-shot
Still in motion.) Arms crossed square, she'd dare;
Staring the camera blind, her heart's fierce fire burning
Somewhere in there, where no draught turned
(And not even x-ray could be unkind.)
    Now time itself blinks
And, maybe, even eternity winks behind
Her famous dark looks and devotion.

Michael Parr

Half a Dozen Gods

Half a dozen gods thought it was about time
they did something, so they packed their bags
and hied them higgledy-piggledy, wives and all,
to the new built city of Tulum. When they got there
it was a tumbledown rack of ruins
hardly what they had been used to,
like the grand hotels at Tikal and Palenque,
not to mention the haciendas of the practical Itzas.
They checked in, grumbling among themselves at the service
which, to say the least, wasn't worth writing home about.
They refused to buy the obligatory postcards lito en Mexico.
I mean, this isn't a nice place to visit
let alone live in and, after all, this is supposed to be
the twilight or dusk or something of the gods
what with the old league falling into decadence
in the worst possible post-classical manner
these organizations seem to need. Anyway, there they were,
disporting themselves like tourists, paying almost nothing
for the great privilege of being waited on hand and foot
—tourists are like that, they say, showing off
and making remarks like "Back home" or "I remember when"
or "This place is nowhere to be caught dead in"

. . . when the distant telegraph announced the arrival
off Isla Mujeres, or was it Cozumel,
of ships packed stem to stern with warriors in helmets,
they were bearded like Snake-Bird,
a sign of two crossed planks made glyphs upon their sails
and they were swearing dreadful oaths to a Santa Maria

—no doubt a woman-god like Ix-Chel, I wouldn't wonder.
Our more-than-a-handful of gods, bored with their vacations,
bestirred themselves at last, expecting some kind of excitement,
and put on their make-up and began to dance in the old
fashioned way
careless of partners or, indeed, careful to manoeuvre each other
so that their own old eyes could look out to sea
—look out to see who it was coming to join their final fling.

Mary Partridge

Vintage

There are some
who come late to poetry
as guests would to dinner
contrite   cautious
unsure of the entree
they offer apology and rose

But you
purple the page
with midwinter plonk
made from fruit
no one else would harvest

Winking
you offer
a jelly-jar salute
and win us over
   with a belch

Mylene Pepin

Behind the Glass

Somewhere between autumn and the glass
are leaves with nowhere to land.
Leaves that clutch the window,
dark and desperate as your hands
that grope for words to fill the night.
Your words, though flakes of sky,
are invisible to the touch.
Your hands, so veined, transparent,
tuck away sounds,
shake at my whispers.
I clothe myself with discarded leaves
and move through you,
unnoticed in the silence.

There is too much silence
in your face webbed against the window,
in the leaves that shine like blades.
Once your cries broke the glass;
the sounds, leaves on water,
spilled into my skin.
I smoothed away your stutters
with the light I strung between my fingers,
felt it vibrate through your limbs.
Once you blazed with autumn's glory
and the wildness deafened me.

H.R. Percy

Soft Core

Once when hurtling
between Howard Johnsons
five over the limit and sandwiched
by many-wheeled monsters
I saw this turtle upturned
like a tureen of itself
and seeming surprised
at the paucity of traction,
as though wound up and abandoned
by some kid whose friend called;
left to run down slowly
and eventually stop
from sheer lack of interest in living.

A few miles farther on for no good reason
a big Mack jack-knifed,
crushed cab and sheeted stretcher
telling the whole story
but staying at any rate
the right way up.

Later that afternoon we paused,
choked down a pun in poor taste
with our quarter-pounder
and soon forgot, as always.

But ceilingward dreaming sometimes
I feel the hard shell forming,
the turnpike's shoulder pushing up

with the dead weight of the world
and hear the tire-swish of eternity.
Among all those wheeling Levites
not one Samaritan and I envy
that teamster's swift oblivion.

Karen Petersen

on the demise of life as we know it

In a week at 2:45 a.m. the world will end.
Damn, didn't even make it to the millennium
that's old Jupiter-cum-Zeus for you
limited sense of history, you know
but heavens (pardon) all of them
ganging up on poor wretched Earth,
we could be a cancer cell the way
they're attacking us like chemotherapy.
Okay, maybe we are a little bit noisy
tossing around all these micro-waves
all the time, not to mention bothering
a couple of our sisters and brothers
with Voyager Is and IIs and so on,
true, we do tend to be a little messy
about all that crap we have in orbit
(no, not you Moon, you don't count,
no, now, don't take it like that. . .)
and we are playing around with all
this nuclear stuff and proton junk
even after Asta of Inter-galactic
Control warned us about it, but
Mercury, show a little compassion
indicative of your caduceus, hey,
and you Venus, show a little love,
and hey Mars. . .oh, never mind. . .
but Jupiter, come now, are you
the mind behind this conspiracy?
And what of you, Saturn, you always
were into overthrow, weren't you?

And Uranus, Neptune and Pluto
most ancient, oceanic, chthonic;
think now about what you're doing.

You don't need another asteroid belt.

Bernadette Rule

The Catch

We walked the seductive curves
of Copacabana and Ipanema,
the licking sea on our right,
a crescent of teeming hotels
on our left. Beyond   at a discreet distance,
cardboard favelas littered the green slopes.

Men from these favelas stood fishing
in the surf. We ducked under
their lines as we passed,
carrying our shoes and wearing the ocean.

At night the favela women
stick candles into the sand
and pray to the sea god
to claim them, flame and all.

The men press the gods by turning around
and throwing their lines
into the hotel windows
which the tourists often leave open
to admit the rare grace
of the warm stars and seasong
of Rio de Janeiro. To hook a purse
or a pair of pants with full pockets
is their humble fisherman's prayer.

We are a curious mix of humanity:
sleeping tourists, silent fishermen

and praying women, and each can feel the gods
hovering in the tropical night
with answers for us all.

Kathy Shaidle

Lead Down the Garden Path
(Riverdale Un-soiled)

Burial.

Camouflage: the art of concealing
   the fact that something has been concealed.

We have been led. To believe.
In the immaculate:
clothes hanging on the line,
defying the death penalty.
In thin dish water, and the curative powers of bleach.
In my grandmother saying
   "No one's too poor to buy soap."
In next-to-godliness.

In Riverdale there are more laundromats than people:
a single sock pinned to a cork board, our flag.
Then why am I awakened by hot tar and an argument?
Why do they wash their cars and believe
that this alone will make them new?

The woman in cinnamon knee-highs on the porch
(the porch still wearing Christmas lights)
believes, but her child is already dirty,
so she knocks his smiling toy
into the front garden
of little tomatoes all holding their breath.
From the garden to the porch
through the hand to the boy—

a path   a line
a trajectory

This morning the city begins digging,
exhuming the invisible.
And the people do not believe,
just keep dragging beer and new fans down the sidewalk.

How to care for people
whose houses are made of potatoes
who eat paint and weeds and bruises
whose dogs laugh at vaccinations
who have never heard of the Roman Empire
who will never read this poem

I don't want to live among these people
    but I'd rather not die among them either
Meantime children run across the playground &
Pigeons fly like bullets,
distant cousins

Naomi Thiers

Elegy for Otto Rene Castillo

Otto Rene Castillo was a Guatemalan poet who lived in exile much of his life because of his political activities. The last time he returned to Guatemala in 1967 he was tortured and burned at the stake by the Guatemalan army. Tecun Uman was a Guatemalan Indian leader also burned at the stake. The italicized words in this poem are from the writings of Otto Rene Castillo.

And the poets of vigorous swords. . .
will know how to love life
where it rises
with its flaming face. . .
because life
is the highest poetry.

In Rio Hondo, in Zacapa
they caught you, Castillo.
They tied your mestizo bones
to a stake in the equatorial
sun. I was ten
when they lit your hair and flamed
what was left of your face.

The eyes of my bones
will be lost in a wind
of ash.

You pressed into my mouth
the bitter earth of Guatemala,
your german wife's hair, and your longing
for corn and clay gods, I eager
to hear you read

Tomorrow, for my joy chiming
in the walls,
the bride will hold her most beautiful bell.

But there was not even a stone for you in Zacapa.
Your blood did not even seed the earth,
only a scar of ashes trailed across scorched gardens.
There was no last poem in your torture.
Peasants saw smoke rising from the mountain
and went on harvesting hunger with machetes.

Little by little we turn
ashen from our skin to our souls.

You knew,
every second of your exile and return,
the exact heat of the grave they had waiting for you

now I am
the skeleton
of a house on fire
that aches inside
a wall of ashes

and what would become of your eyes.
But your pen cut Mayan stone.
Your tongue released the red fire bound
since Tecun Uman in a husk of corn.

Kathleen Thomson

Saskatchewan 1933

emma was a bride
and young like a colt
when the prairie dust
settled like a blood leech
on saskatchewan,
on thigh and throat,
and the ventricles of her heart
bewildered
still beat:
two moth wings,
singed.

emma's hair
was a harvest of wheat
and her lips stained her face
like berry juice,
but in the mirror
her hope grew
stunted and strange,
and her husband
in his cotton shirt
wandered in rooms,
as in a maze.

emma pressed her lips
to the porch screen
and dreamed of Ontario
and the bright plumage
of birds in wet meadows;

of the tender breasts,
the clear, white milk
of the wetnurse;
of the sermon on the mount
and the disciples feeding
multitudes.

emma and the farm pharaohs
had dust in their pockets
and locusts on their brows,
but the silt of saskatchewan
lay on home and hearth
and muddied dreams
and emma,
burning on the prairie
like a match girl,
lay in the sheets at night
with her harvest hair
and spat out her youth
in tiny flames.

Sarah Tolmie

The Salmon of Knowledge

Cuculainn crouched by the dark streamside
fishing with a bronze hook
for the salmon of knowledge
he baited his hook with small things
ticks from his dogs, and grubs
small rodents he found in the woods
for a long time
he fished, and the salmon would not come
then it rose up, and grabbed the bait
and sank without a trace
the bronze hook floated empty
Cuculainn tried larger bait
he caught a wild boar
and threw it into the stream
attached to the bronze hook
the salmon craned its mouth just half open
and swallowed it whole
he was old and wise and slippery
the bronze hook floated empty
Cuculainn became desperate
he hurled in his shining torc
and seized great clods of earth
to bait the bronze hook
the salmon ate it all
and was not caught
but with every bite it grew bigger
Cuculainn was frenzied
he offered still larger bait
small towns, church spires

the salmon rolled its eye and splashed
devoured the towns and spires
with undisturbed digestion
and all the while it grew
Cuculainn, who was brave
but ignorant
did not get out of the way in time
as the bloated salmon
outgrew the riverbed
stretching and slithering
it slid across continents
crushing the uninformed in its path
Cuculainn was not the first to try to catch it
but a bronze hook is not strong enough
Cuculainn is long dead
but the salmon of knowledge is still loose
with one wallop of its wet, smacking tail
it could kill us all

Daniel Treisman

Silvana Dancing

Two steps forward, one step back.
Eyes closed, lost to your partner,
you cross the floor and exit into Africa,

Peace Corps-ing round the world,
unglobing it. What I admired
was how your bore your centre with you,

teasing gravity with the bravado
of a gyroscope, stepping out
of circles, changing your mind.

May the motion last a while.
And when, eyes ready and surprised,
you tiptoe back

towards our
world of anchored orbits,
may the stillness do no injury.

M. Tropp

Poet To Poet
for Arthur Rimbaud

Songs and shoats and drunken boats
Rimbaud's hell is out of season

Does he care. . .? "I'm never there,"
He tries to tell his father's guests

The tears of sister raise a blister
On the sacred statuary

Flowers and evil in upheaval
And every day is out of key

Rimbaud clings to honey-bee stings
As if his fate was accompli

Rimbaud knows, on all ten toes
How mathematics edifies

Still—he reels, strips and kneels
Swabs his passion with absinthe

And every sin is where he's been
. . . fin de siecle, fin de Rimbaud!

Jan Truss

Legal Separation

He has taken his death away from me
After fifteen sick years of hospital promises
I'd always assumed he'd die for me
Leave me to mourn
But he has taken his promise
Run away with it
Rejoicing like a youth set free
To woo and wander.

Shall I rejoice or mourn?

"I would have died for you," he told me
When he'd decided not to.
He moved out
Taking his death with him
A gift for somebody else.

Christl Verduyn

Writing women

nightly

i wait

in the cemetery
for   the space
men   to come

at dusk   i dig
up the bones
i've carefully picked
clean and polished
smooth as stone
and lay them   lovingly
end to end
in great sprawling
words to woo men
down from the night skies

i wait
for a searching
beacon to pick out
my signal

i sit
in a circle of shining skulls
with welcoming smiles
beckoning star
men

i am calm
and daily more confident
that the night is soon now
when stones   bones   men and i
will be sucked   spiralling
into the sky

N. von Maltzahn

Country preaching

Touched with a taste for divinity,
a young minister preaches to an old parish

in his white church, where the road leaves the sea.
A summer morning brings neither the young nor the dead

on whatever a Sunday of Pentecost,
but the old, mostly women, careful, with hats.

As a student he had stumbled in the city,
tongue hampered as a trotter, drink after drink;

in three-o-clock sun on Gottingen Street
a saint of the Irish spoke his own language—

saint of old gratitude now found in undress,
with all a tree's need for forgiveness—

in a brown suit, dirt bled to his collar tip,
slumping on a Pontiac's uncasual green.

Etherized, they each blinked in the light.
There came an end to his student charity.

Faced again with the choice of lives,
who would choose as he has chosen, who would not?

Unexaminable lives! Was his interest
in men or in man? What was his language?

So he preaches a holy ghostly prodigy or prophecy,
a glory in the mists of Aspotogan,

or at last a low comedy, seals barking
idle salutes to a new tide.

Bill Wilson

Close Encounter with a Red-Winged Blackbird

Flushed a red-winged blackbird
when I was out visiting some trees.
Stood right over me, on the phone
calling his lawyer, badmouthing me
to his kids. He's a family man.

Up in a dead tree, a hawk
reads the menu. Leftover stew
of nosey rodents. The maitre'd
asks me to leave but in a nice way.
It's a busy day and the lady's
an old customer.

Conceding that everybody
has to eat, I try a homily.
"Fellows, God loves you but
the neighbourhood's changing
and the owner is just waiting
for his price. Try to see
the big picture." It works.

And now, sitting here
with my last Golden of the day,
it occurs to me
that after many a summer dies the swan
and I feel the hush
that's all over the world and wait
for Sunday when I can think
how truly great

Jack Ham has been over the years
against the pass
and against the rush.

Doreen Wilson

Listen Angels

Listen, Angels
You stand near the Door.
You watch fools.
You black-browed Angels!
You purse-lipped Angels!
Listen, You unkissed Angels!
Listen, You.
You, trembling
        on thresholds
Wings folded, you watch.
You follow this fool's
        joyous flight
through heavy doors
        towards the light.

O if I could, I would loosen,
                loosen gently
every feathered wing
and fly you toward
that bright and shining
                Space
    in which I Sing.

Ilanna Yuditsky

Jihad

Holy wars fought to protect a promise
            of land and sea

Children cry mournful tears   in white stone houses
now reduced to rubble   by foreign made tanks.

Their damp eyes search ever-present cameras
for an answer   to their bloodshed.
They are frightened.

Streets rage with bullets in the night
Black-robed mothers wail for their sons,
unwilling recruits
            to an international scheme of terror

For them
        without their sons
            there will be no tomorrow

Today the guns cease   it is a holiday

The space is filled with silence
Yet even in silence
        there
          is
            no
              peace.